EMBRACING
Southern
HOMES

ERIC ROSS

Gibbs Smith

"By wisdom a house is built,
and through understanding it is established;
through knowledge its rooms are filled
with rare and beautiful treasures."

Proverbs 24:3–4

CONTENTS

A SOUTHERN WELCOME   9

FRENCH FORMALITY   13

A GENTLEMAN FARMER'S MILIEU   35

REFINING MANOR   55

ELEGANT LEGACY   69

MID-ATLANTIC SOLITUDE   97

LONE STAR SHOWCASE   115

URBAN RESTRAINT   127

AMONG THE LIVE OAKS   141

COLONIAL ALLURE   155

CREATING ELAN   169

BRIGHT ON THE WATER   187

A PASTORAL VISION   207

A SOUTHERN WELCOME

When I think of the importance of home, especially the Southern home, I'm flooded with memories. Large parties that my wife, Ruthann, and I have hosted always bring a smile as I think of old friends and our times together. Intimate dinners prepared for special occasions with friends and family bring a familiar sense of warmth and memories of the good times we shared. Our gatherings can be grand or intimate. Something as simple as a last-minute evening gathering by the fire for cocktails or catching up with dear friends at a moment's notice can provide surprise and relief from an otherwise dreary day. Impromptu gatherings are often some of our best parties! Yet no matter the occasion, the one constant in all of these events is our Southern home. Our home is the centerpiece to some of the most important events in our lives. The age-old tradition of hosting friends and family is the best way to show hospitality—encompassing love and goodwill for those in our lives who are important to us.

It is no surprise that a Southern home is so universally admired for the way it makes its visitors feel. The lush and layered interiors that are a hallmark of Southern homes provide a warm and inviting tableau for hosting guests. A traditional Southern room creates a sense of stability, heritage, and warmth. In every area of the country, many people admire the enduring nature of rooms filled with lavish fabrics and antiques.

But what is it that makes Southern homes and the rooms within them so special? Just as a recipe takes essential ingredients to create a gourmet dish, there are several essential elements that make up the idealized Southern home. These rooms are typically planned with deep, ample seating upholstered in sumptuous fabrics in a myriad of colors and textures. Antiques and heirlooms are another important part of the Southern design aesthetic. Antiques are not just beautiful because of the patina of time, but also for the stories they tell. The family histories are told and retold as guests return again and again to a room which displays family art and collectibles. These items can manifest the spirit of times past and hearken to a slower, more refined pace of life. They bring to life the romance of a bygone era. Another integral ingredient to the Southern home is the window treatments. In my view, window treatments are the most important element. Fabric curtains are a key component to creating a captivating room; fabric not only creates an essential visual backdrop to rooms but is an important sound absorber and effective method for light control and privacy. Traditionally, curtains can be long side panels designed with complicated top treatments with swags and jabots to create a theatrical effect. However, today's Southern interiors rely more on simple pleated drapes with complementary soft Roman shades or even custom-built louvered shutters. The effect is not only dramatic, but less intimidating for today's more relaxed living.

What is it I am really trying to say about Southern homes and the rooms in which we live? Southern homes have an essence, a feeling to them that many people outside of the South are drawn to. The interiors of the South have a history, approachability, and comfort. These rooms embrace you. I noted some key elements that create a Southern room, but what really makes it so special is that every room tells a story. The romance of the South combines struggle, grit, tradition, and style. French, Spanish, English, and Native American people have each left their mark on the style and spirit that is the American South—it is reflected in the architecture and interiors throughout the region. The effort to blend these styles is not intended as a history lesson, but rather to create a European inspired eclecticism that communicates both ease and refinement. That is the essence of a Southern room.

Southern rooms are also rich with details. A heavy use of textiles, color, and a variety of wood finishes gives character and contrast among all the different materials in a room. This allows the visitor to any Southern room to discover unique and different aspects of the interiors every time they visit. Sometimes one notices an antique textile used on a pillow; the next time they will notice a beautiful hand-blocked fabric on a chair or wool blanket that makes them warm and comfortable. These unique and artisanal touches add character and animate many Southern interiors making them memorable; they entice visitors to return again and again. The well-thought-out combination of items, in the end, creates a recipe for fine living.

In recent years, people nationwide have desired more meaningful interiors for themselves and those they love. From Maryland to Texas, I have found new clients eager to apply all the qualities I have described in the Southern home aesthetic to their homes—regardless of whether they live in the South. Social media is such an effective tool for my firm, Eric Ross Interiors, as it allows me to introduce my sense of Southern style to clients across the country and has connected me to people I would not have had the opportunity to work with otherwise. A client from Minnesota, who spent many years in Georgia, longed to reconnect with her memories from her Southern past. So, she asked me to create some rooms for her home in the northern U.S. A client from Tennessee wanted a coastal home in Maryland decorated in a Southern manner. A Texas resident contacted me to make his home in Texas feel as special as his sister's home I designed and decorated in South Carolina. I have even completed one modern project to show my take on modern style in the South. All these projects originated from a desire to have a bit of the seemingly familiar Southern style in one's home.

Welcome to my newest collection of recently completed homes collected from across the South. I am happy to share these interiors with you, to show how I introduced these families to the joy of living with the things they love. If you have read my previous book, *Enduring Southern Homes*, or follow me on social media, you know I relish curating rooms for clients and friends where they can share the most important days—and even the most unimportant days—of their lives, with others. These new spaces are Southern rooms in their enduring style and quality that sets them apart from the ordinary. They are decorated to set the stage for welcoming family and friends into homes that are designed from a legacy of elegant Southern living.

OPPOSITE: A painting by a family friend adorns the mantel of a romantic farmhouse in rural Tennessee, complementing the blue-and-green color scheme in the home. Modern-style wing chairs look perfectly at home nestled around the fireplace featuring small-honed natural slate tile.

FRENCH FORMALITY

This project came at a time when I was the busiest I had ever been, and I didn't have room in my schedule for one more. But it was a perfect fit for me, so I just had to make room. The clients were moving to Nashville, having lived in California, Connecticut, and Florida. After selling their furnishings with their previous house, they requested all new furnishings and window treatments for their entirely new home in Tennessee. They were well traveled and loved a traditional style of decorating and living. I was hired in July with one stipulation: most of the work had to be installed by Christmas. I was excited to see what we could do together.

The house was a French chateau style in stone, complete with a bridge over a ravine that becomes a moat during heavy rainstorms. The setting, with mature trees and ample acreage, appeared like something out of a movie set. One reason I accepted this project was its location. Not only was it beautiful, but it was within two miles of my home and studio. The proximity would help with time management, and I would easily be able to check on progress as we installed wallcoverings and repainted. Another reason it appealed to me was that it was just a redecorating project. When I say "just," what I mean is that we didn't have to tear down walls or retile or refinish anything. The focus was on new paint on the exterior and interior, and on redecorating the entire house.

To begin with, the exterior trim color was white, which didn't contribute to the house looking soft and aged. I shy away from white, in general, because it is harsh and feels too new in most settings. So, I selected a gray-green color to soften the eaves, over-hangs, and windows, allowing them to blend into the stonework. This made the mass of the house feel older and more established. The clients refreshed the landscape and added pink crepe myrtle to give a jolt of color and lend softness to the façade.

When I first toured the interior of the home, a truffle brown wall color saturated the majority of the first and second floors. Ten thousand square feet of truffle is a lot of brown! All this darkness gave the interiors a rather gloomy disposition. The antidote: adding a lot of color and pattern. Injecting bold color and pattern in the two-story foyer cut through the murky environment. There was ample natural light from windows in the foyer and coming from the upper gallery. The scale of the room was grand—using a standard wallcovering or paint would have been too plain for such a large space. My inspiration for the room was to create the look of a conservatory with lots of color and movement. A sense of movement is particularly important in foyers and hallways because you want people to move through these spaces.

To the left of the foyer is the music room with walls clad in a cognac-color paneled wood and a black painted ceiling; both finishes were preexisting. I placed the clients' black baby grand piano in this room to repeat the black of the ceiling. Fortuitously, the wood panels in combination with the double-height ceiling created ideal acoustics for the piano. A lush, embroidered drapery fabric became the centerpiece of my design for the study. The cognac-colored flower in the fabric was a perfect match to

ABOVE: A charming bronze figure adorns a French chest in the dining room.

OPPOSITE: The dining room's design culminated in the client contributing a pair of monumental cut-glass urns in amber that are the centerpieces of the room.

the walls, and I finished the color scheme with dark lichen and cream to create a paradoxically restful and dramatic room.

The dining room had a traditional large-scale damask wallcovering in yellow and parchment, which established a classic background for one of the few pieces the clients brought to the project: a custom-made oval dining table in walnut. I added new scalloped-back dining chairs in a red cut velvet that resembles small feathers. For draperies, I designed a dramatic combination of deep green and yellow fabrics with traditional swags and jabots accompanied by a faux Roman shade in a quintessential chinoiserie pattern colored in jewel tones.

The formal salon was situated in the center of the manse. This central great room featured an oval gallery that surrounded the upper floor looking down to the center of the salon. I chose to arrange the furnishings in mirror images on either end of the room in order to take advantage of the views of the pool and rear loggia. This also allowed for more space in the center of the room. The furniture was arranged to allow one to enjoy views of both inside and out, as well as letting in the most possible daylight. In this case, I kept the truffle brown walls as a foil against light fabrics and carpeting. A custom cut and bound area rug enhanced the architectural outline of the space and kept a cleaner look for the grand room.

Some of my favorite rooms in the house were in the primary bedroom wing. The entry room to the wing was a turreted room with five windows that offered such pretty views of the grounds. I covered the walls in a subtle cameo-colored watermark fabric and enhanced it with a crabapple blossom fabric in white with chocolate embroidery. I covered the chairs and skirted table all in the same fabric, which repeated the tree branches from the outdoors. This quiet and elegant tableau created a relaxing visual palette before entering the sleeping chamber. The sleeping chamber showcased a blue woven pattern in linen on walls, windows, and upholstery.

Upstairs the home has four large guest bedrooms. When I have homes with this many bedrooms, I like to create stories about the people who may be using these rooms to inspire me. For this home, we had an all blue-and-white bedroom for a gentleman. One bedroom was a French-style lady's bedroom with creams and teal. Another bedroom had terra-cotta and brown, so I named it the Sedona bedroom. Finally, the fourth bedroom I named the Russian Presidential Suite. I used red and pink as a strong color combination in this room with very elegant fabrics and furnishings. Each room had its own personality, but the common theme was formality and strong color.

This house is one of my favorite projects and also one I am most proud of, not only for the final look, but also because we were able to install a majority of it by our Christmas deadline. I was able to use some of my favorite design motifs, such as birds and flowers, as well as loads of color and formality. I love dressy and elegant rooms, but usually have to restrain myself from making them too fussy. Thankfully, these clients asked for even more formality to the rooms. The final outcome of this home demonstrated how formal and elegant can also be warm and delightful.

OPPOSITE: The elaborately paneled music room stained in cognac is the perfect backdrop for the lively embroidered drapery panels. Accents of charcoal and olive create a dramatic effect in the room.

OPPOSITE: The serpentine back of the chairs creates a lyrical environment for listening to music before and after dinner.

ABOVE: A baby grand piano is positioned in the corner to allow for more seating in the music room. A gold-colored, faux bamboo cocktail table is centered between two chairs and a French-style settee. A great seating arrangement always has a place to set a drink while guests visit each other.

OVERLEAF: The painterly bird-and-branch motif silk fabric for the grand salon's window treatments provides luster and elegance. To fill the large grand salon, a pair of ample seating areas provides views out to the piazza beyond.

ABOVE: Both sides of the grand salon feature sitting areas that include velvet sofas and Italian-style mirrors with a collection of chinoiserie watercolors painted on rice paper.

OPPOSITE: The upper gallery is the perfect area to showcase the homeowners' art collection. An elaborate artisan railing in black iron crowns the grand salon below. The shape of the iron chandelier fits perfectly in the center of the gallery and the room below it.

A collection of European cityscapes inspire the color scheme in the den. Dark green velvet sofas are a favorite of mine and here wool plaid pairs perfectly with a cocktail ottoman with exquisitely carved lion's feet and nailhead trim.

ABOVE: The clients' collection of blue-and-white Chinese export porcelain is the perfect foil to a dark mahogany table in the upper gallery of the home.

OPPOSITE: I often use one fabric *en masse* in bedrooms, especially because it creates both a dramatic but also relaxing environment.

LEFT: Blue and white is always right. Here, an ikat stripe wallcovering gives vitality to a guest bedroom. Known as the Blue Bedroom, for obvious reasons, the clients' vintage collection of English bachelor prints feels perfectly at home here.

ABOVE: This blue velvet chair creates a cozy corner for guests to relax or a spot to sit while putting on shoes before heading out for adventure.

RIGHT: A jardiniere the client owned before the project finds the perfect home between two large French doors draped in curtains of brightly colored embroidered flowers.

BELOW: The client had a collection of rugs when we began the project, including this French-style Aubusson rug in pinks and reds. To embrace the color scheme, pink grass cloth covers the walls and red velvet adorns the sofa.

OPPOSITE: A Russian aesthetic is the inspiration for this guest bedroom and this Russian-style armchair reinforces the look in the sitting area to great effect. The client has an extensive collection of red crystal and much of it lives nicely in this room.

ABOVE: The primary suite has the same fabric on the walls, bed, sofa, and window treatments. There is a serenity to blue and a formality to damask that translates well in such a room as this.

OPPOSITE: Vignette arrangements throughout the main suite create a serene, elegant environment in this part of the home.

A GENTLEMAN FARMER'S MILIEU

CLARKSVILLE, TENNESSEE

"Dream project" is a phrase that I am questioned about often. Whether I am interviewing with the media about my work or discussing projects with fellow designers, I am asked, "What is your dream project?" or "Do you have any dream projects coming up?" While all of my interior design projects are interesting in their own way, not all of them fall into the category of a dream project. As I look at my portfolio of work, many of my projects are what I call bread and butter to my business—they pay the bills. A living room this month, a bedroom next month, these projects are fun and rewarding to see come to life, but aren't dream worthy. So, when I was approached by a young, professional couple to help them develop and create a farm estate north of Nashville, I jumped at the chance to guide them. This project was the stuff dream projects are made of.

Designing a custom home and floor plan is always a daunting task. These clients had never built a home, let alone a series of buildings and supporting farm structures. They had many questions and uncertainties regarding interior layouts. They wanted to suit their family's needs while also optimizing the use of the land. It took several months to work out the final floor plan for the main house alone. Originally, I was hired to help them build the main house on the property. But as we worked on creating floor plans and building elevations, developing fifty acres of land, and siting the house with the main drive to access and connect all of these structures, we decided it would be best to start with the smaller guesthouse

and retreat barn. This would provide a learning curve and some experience for the couple, who also had two small children at the time. Once we decided to start the project by building the guesthouse, the clients didn't want to wait for several months to develop a floor plan. So, we decided to purchase a stock floor plan from a home plan website and tweak the layout to our needs. Buying a stock floor plan did save time and money because it gave us a framework—we weren't starting from scratch. In half the time originally anticipated, we were ready to break ground.

While my team was working on redesigns and changes to the guesthouse, the clients and I had many meetings on site locating all the future buildings. One of my favorite memories was discussing where to locate the main drive. The husband wanted to put a road straight up the hill to the top of the property where the manor house would eventually sit. I thought this was a missed opportunity. The land boasts a creek that winds along the north of the property. A bridge would have to be built to cross the creek to provide access to the rest of the land. So, I suggested we have the road cross the creek and then gently turn to follow its winding path. This would allow visitors to meander along the creek until the drive turns again to surmount the grassy knoll. Of course, this would add more length to the drive and cost. He didn't like the impact to the budget. I responded, "You've bought fifty acres, you need to show off the fifty acres before visitors get to

the house. It's impressive." In the end, he agreed—and still continues to remind me of the cost. But the cost was worth it because the drive now makes a romantic and restful experience for all who come onto the farm.

The clients had a wish list of three structures that would eventually sit on the property. They wanted a large barn that would house the husband's extensive car collection and provide a retreat area for family and friends. The retreat area of the barn would accommodate a living room and dining room, as well as a full bath and kitchenette. They wanted the three-bedroom guesthouse. And, finally, they wanted the manor house. A vegetable and cutting garden was also desired. During our dreaming and discussions, we decided to name the farm Highfields, because the land sits up on a high rise of acreage overlooking other middle Tennessee farmland. The views are very special, and the name fits the land perfectly. At times guests can feel like they are above the clouds.

After all of the vision casting at the beginning of the project, I was eager to begin the construction and finish selections process. We all agreed the guesthouse should be charming and look as if it had been on the property for 100 years. The husband was very involved in the look of the interiors. An avid reader of books on manor houses and the history of gentleman farmers and their homes, he sent me many pictures of architectural elements along with notes that he wanted to incorporate. We decided a more cottage-style guesthouse in the vernacular form would be appropriate for a farm in Tennessee. The backstory we created was the guesthouse was the original home on the farmstead

with the barn and its expansion built over time. This backstory also gives the new property a sense of history and purpose.

The guesthouse was small—approximately 2,400 square feet. Upon entering the sparse foyer with a small, attached powder room, you walked into an open kitchen and living room. The primary bedroom and bathroom rounded out the main floor. Upstairs featured two small bedrooms separated by a sitting room used as a playroom area and a full bath that both children shared. Because the house wasn't huge, I chose neutral colors and fabrics throughout to give more continuity and trick the eye into thinking the interiors were larger.

Another part of this project included designing and building a retreat barn. Originally envisioned as a place to house the husband's burgeoning car collection, the vision for the barn expanded into a space that would also include gathering and entertaining spaces. Because the guesthouse had only one living room, we decided to include a large gathering room, dining room, and home office to give the family some elbow room. We also included a full bath and kitchenette. The couple wanted to be able to accommodate large parties inside or outside, so an ancillary open carport area originally meant for tractor storage became outdoor living space as well.

As you enter the foyer to the living spaces in the retreat barn, I repeated the same colors that were used in the guesthouse. Shades of olive, sage, and basil adorned the walls and trim. We displayed handsome wildlife trophies and plates on a small-patterned wallcovering to give vintage appeal to guests as they enter. It evokes the feeling of "we celebrate farm life" in this room.

PRECEDING OVERLEAF: The retreat barn is designed to hold large gatherings of family and friends.

OPPOSITE: One end of the retreat barn houses a kitchenette with ample refreshments at the ready for parties of every kind.

The gathering room had vast vaulted ceilings and could be used for various functions. On one side of the room was the ample sitting area. Two sofas faced each other, flanking the large screen television. I designed two handsome leather-topped cocktail ottomans with trays to be used for drinks. The sofas and chairs in this room were covered in an outdoor fabric in shades of tobacco and cognac. A large area rug was topped with a smaller antique Persian rug to outline the seating arrangement.

On the opposite side of the gathering room was the dining area. A ten-foot dining table anchored this space with a combination of dining chair styles. I selected a dynamic and colorful ikat print for the windows to create a sense of drama against the soft sage walls. The real centerpiece of this area was the pair of bronze elk statuary that rested in the center of the dining table. They reinforced the rugged yet refined nature of the barn and property.

At the far end of the gathering room, a pair of rugged barn doors allowed access to the home office that the husband used daily. He requested a dedicated office space apart from the main home when he, or his wife, needed to work in a quiet environment. This room was replete with bookcases for storage and display of family photos and artifacts. I tucked a small sofa into the room for napping when needed on lazy afternoons. All the colors and finishes in this room also continued the soft greens echoed throughout the property, hearkening to the natural aspects of rural living.

The outdoor living area was exceptionally large in order to accommodate considerable-sized parties. I designed two ample seating areas in this space as well as a twelve-foot dining table. On one side of the seating area, I placed a charming bed swing with iron rods for hanging rather than chain. The iron rods provide more stability in the wind and add a rustic element to the design. For the opposite side of the outdoor seating area, I found a primitive-style teak sofa that looks perfect on the farm and nicely anchors the seating group. For the outdoor dining area, favorite chairs in a combination of iron and what looks like rush weaving (but is resin) sat around the dining table. The resin is actually PVC material that is weatherproof. Various fabrics in mustard, white, and honey tones rounded out the multiple seating areas.

Not only was this a rewarding project because it sharpened my skills in land development as well as architectural design, but it also allowed me to see how one's plans could change over time. What started as a project to design and build a large manor house turned into designing and decorating ancillary farm buildings. Learning to hone the property and natural landscape in order to prepare for more fully developed plans in the future was an inspiring adventure for me and my clients. I have gained two great friends who will be working with me for many years to come as we dream, design, and build the various living spaces and supportive structures on their farm at Highfields.

OPPOSITE: The retreat barn showcases a variety of areas to relax, eat, watch TV, or read a book.

The living room features a custom mantel with a small carved antique cartouche I found at an antique show and purchased for this project. It depicts a fox hunting a rabbit hiding from its hunter. I designed the mantelpiece to feature the cartouche in the center. The mantel is really the centerpiece of the room and cottage, so we decided to name the cottage The Fox and Rabbit.

ABOVE: The clients have a love of collecting, as I do. Here it is fun to display a small collection of oyster plates on the wall of their living room.

OPPOSITE: The window treatments in the living room are a lively vine print with embroidery accents. This gives the room an elevated feel, even though the cottage is in the countryside.

OPPOSITE: Because the cottage is a small house with space at a minimum, the kitchen table is located against a window and can be pulled out to accommodate larger parties when the need arises. The contrast of black chairs against the white table is a classic combination that never fails.

ABOVE: Two shades of green cover the kitchen cabinets: sage and basil. I like to use food names when describing colors that I use in interior design as it conjures more of a visual image for the clients.

OPPOSITE: The primary bedroom showcases hushed tones of white and cashew. I found a small floral-and-vine motif print and used it on the draperies and repeated it on the bedding. I selected a modern, pixelated flame-stitch fabric that hearkens to old quilting patterns and topped the bed with a matelassé coverlet for easy cleaning.

The bed is a black spindle style, and the rest of the case goods are in bleached wood, which keeps the room light and fresh. On the wall above the bed is my hallmark arrangement of dishes, which I often display on walls as a collection of art.

ABOVE: The primary bath is short on space but big on charm. A slate floor gives a sense of rusticity and texture, perfect for a farm cottage.

ABOVE AND OPPOSITE: The foyer of the cottage features a large-scale print of pomegranate trees in black and gold. The effect is similar to hand stenciling. I like the primitive quality this gives to set the tone of the interior design scheme.

OVERLEAF: The exterior porch of the retreat barn has panoramic views of middle Tennessee. The faux rush furniture is the perfect accompaniment to the rustic and elegant space.

REFINING MANOR

GREEN HILLS, TENNESSEE

The power of social media, particularly Instagram, as a means to attract new clients has been one of the biggest surprises of my career. My wife, Ruthann, suggested that we do a weekly series showcasing what happens behind the scenes in our design studio. We both realized very quickly that this was an excellent way to attract potential new clients. Within the first several months of the behind-the-scenes series, I had new clients from across the United States. Surprisingly, only one was from my home base of Nashville, Tennessee.

Located on one of the most coveted streets in Green Hills—a street lined with mature trees and old, heritage-era houses—this home was built in the 1920s. As I drove up the long gravel drive, I was excited to see what rooms lay behind the imposing red brick façade. Upon entering the home, I was pleased to see a central entry hall that ran the entire depth of the house. This is a favorite architectural feature of mine for many reasons. One is that it allows a visual connection to the rear of the house from the moment you walk in the door, creating vast sight lines. This augments the sense of space. Another reason I love a central hallway is that the windows on the far end allow for more natural light. Natural light is better than artificial light because it brings a sense of life and dynamic energy to interiors. A central hallway can also provide a sense of formality that will create the perfect atmosphere for a receiving hall for guests.

For the foyer hall, I immediately knew I wanted to use a hand-painted Chinese wallcovering. The magic with a hand-painted wallcovering is that you can work with the exact scale of the walls and ceiling in a room. The wallcovering in the studio enlarges or reduces the scale of flora and fauna in the design scheme as well as add varying types of birds, flowers, and even insects—it is truly custom. For this house, I used the wallcovering throughout the entire foyer hall, from the front door continuing up the staircase and finishing on the mezzanine level. This allowed for an eighteen-foot expanse of paper flowing from the base of the stairs to the ceiling on the second floor—a grand statement to behold. Another decision in designing the wallcovering was to use a sepia-tone color palette in shades of parchment, taupe, and brown. This gave the floral design a more tranquil feeling than if it were rendered in polychrome. I make it a practice when I use a lot of something—whether it is two-story draperies or 100 yards of wallcovering—to keep it in a neutral color pallet. This makes it easier to live with over time, and this foyer hall was no different. Also, every other room in the house flowed from this central hall, so a neutral scheme allowed more ease in designing the other rooms.

As you enter the living room, the clients' extensive collection of existing French antiques was highlighted. Sitting rooms, whether formal or casual, should be approachable and relatable, not just to the client, but to their guests as well. This room was no exception. The French antiques inherently felt more feminine because of their scale and high ornamentation. The clients' collection included intricately carved floor lamps, several tables, a chest, and various styles of portraiture along with the centerpiece

PRECEDING OVERLEAF: People intrinsically expect foyers to be more formal. That is why I like to create dramatic and elegant moments in these spaces and use the opportunity to make more of a fuss, if you will, using formal fabrics and wall finishes. Because a foyer is not really a room guests will sit in, guests being uneasy with the formality is not a concern.

An elegant, hand-painted wallcovering by Gracie Studios is the perfect backdrop to a skirted table covered in a pinstripe chintz accented with bullion fringe located in the foyer hall. The top of the table is layered in blue-and-white Chinese export porcelain, another hallmark of my design work.

RIGHT: I don't love leather but I do use it on chairs quite a bit for texture. Leather is slippery and cold to me. To help combat this effect, I like to use seat cushions in fabric, which also adds a decorative effect.

of the room, which showcased a framed tapestry of a cherub surrounded by flora. The Turkish-style rugs were pink and brown. All of these pieces combined felt a little too precious. I wanted to tighten up the flouncy feeling of the room and make it a little more tailored and masculine. To that end, I selected large-scale upholstery and heavily textured fabrics in cream, brown, and cognac with pale blue accents. The scale of the sofa and chairs, along with the heavy-weight fabrics, gave a masculine heft to balance the feminine lightness of the other objets d'art.

If the living room was originally overly feminine, the kitchen was the opposite. The cabinets were black with white marble counters, and the floors were reclaimed brick laid in a herringbone pattern. These finishes were stunning, but also very visually heavy. There were no upper cabinets along the exterior wall due to the ample placement of windows—this created another problem. The room was west facing so the sun was overbearing in the afternoon. That much glare from the sun can make a room difficult to use. One trick I use in rooms with too much natural light is to use dark colors on the walls. Dark colors absorb light rather than reflect it. So, I selected a dark green and black sisal wallcovering with a straw-colored accent. I pulled this straw color to use as a feminine foil to the other dark finishes.

The client had remodeled the primary bedroom and bathroom several years ago, so she requested that I just redecorate with new fabrics and finishes.

I selected new bedding, window treatments, and carpets for these areas. I found a soft, pretty string cloth in celadon for the bedroom walls and a delicate, large-scale, pink and brown warp-dyed Jacobean floral fabric to use as a dramatic counterpoint to the soft palette of the room. The room wasn't large enough for a sitting area, so I found a petite bench with a tufted back that gave the feeling of a small sofa. It fooled the eye, giving the room more prominence than if it didn't have the additional settee.

Across the hall from the primary bedroom is the grandchildren's bedroom. This was such a treat to design because the client found the most precious French-style twin beds to incorporate into the design. I wanted the room to have a bit of whimsy and youthfulness. To that end, I wallpapered the ceiling in a modernized latticework and found a busy and loud print in chocolate, raspberry, and key lime green to display on Roman shades and pillows. The center of the pattern reminded me of an ice cream cone, which I thought was a fun nod to childhood—what child doesn't like ice cream?

Being asked to design and decorate a house on one of our most cherished and historic streets in Nashville was one of my dream projects. In a city that is continually changing and disposing of the old to make way for the new, I am happy to know that I contributed a traditional and long-lasting style to this Southern home.

OPPOSITE: The client loves French interiors, so on this end of the large living room we placed a fantastic French-style daybed. A tapestry already owned by the client when we started the project, featuring flowers and a cherub, takes center stage. Very French.

OPPOSITE AND ABOVE: The keeping room features a pretty and delicate cotton floral with accents of straw yellow for swivel chairs and the same fabric for the valances on the windows in the kitchen area.

Because the client didn't want a dedicated breakfast room, I tucked a small breakfast table in the corner of the keeping room. This allows the family to eat at a table rather than the built-in counter when desired.

RIGHT: More French-style accents in the primary suite. The wall panels are of a pastoral scene in bright colors of celadon and pink.

BELOW: Pink and green is a pretty color combination, so when I found this warp-dyed print of large India-inspired flowers I knew it would be a great addition to this bedroom. The brown in the print keeps it from being overly feminine.

OPPOSITE: The client has wonderful antiques throughout the house. This highly flourished French floor lamp looks ideal among the soft green walls and window treatments.

LEFT AND ABOVE: A pair of child-sized slipper chairs in a combination of French knot embroidery and ticking stripe sit at the foot of the beds, rather than a stool. These small chairs can be used by children to sit on or as a place for their overnight bag for easy accessibility.

I found a sweet set of antique majolica in green, white, and purple to display on the walls with brackets and foo dogs. All of these items finish the room and tie in the color from the fabric on the windows and bedding.

ELEGANT LEGACY

MURFREESBORO, TENNESSEE

The most wonderful couple contacted our firm to help them design and decorate their new construction project, which would be their primary residence. Sometimes it can take a while to get in the groove with a new client so we both feel comfortable discussing the likes and dislikes for a project. But this time, the clients quickly became new friends.

Their house would be built in the neighborhood of a small community approximately forty minutes outside of Nashville. They came to the project with an existing floor-plan already developed by an architect, however they had a few changes they wanted to make to the main kitchen. They also wanted to add more classical trim details inside the home. For this, I contacted the much sought-after James Dunn, owner of Vintage Millworks, based in Nashville, to work with me to create elegant and dramatic trim details throughout the home. The house itself was more than 10,000 square feet including outdoor living spaces. When you have a project of this size, clear and repeated communication is vital for success. I knew having a project manager from our firm would be necessary for this project so that if one of us couldn't make it to the site at a moment's notice, the other one could.

Once we got the layout of the rooms correct and the architecture refined to a more traditionally elegant interior, I began working on the furnishings and finishes. The first thing the homeowners and I agreed we wanted for the home was a mural wallcovering in the dining room. My inspiration for the dining room was an Irish manor house with heavy moldings and a crystal chandelier. In my mind, a pastoral scenic wallcovering would be the perfect foil to the refinement of the millwork and crystal.

Across the hall from the dining room was a gentleman's study. I painted the walls in a bold peacock blue and papered the ceiling in 24-karat gold-leaf paper. Originally, the plan was to lacquer the room in the peacock blue color, but I decided this was too trendy for the long term. The room was large enough to arrange a sitting area at one end and a desk at the other. In a nod to English tradition, I selected a large-scale wool paisley fabric to dress the windows, chairs, and pillows.

Moving through the grand stair hall, one is welcomed into the heart of the home—the living room and open kitchen. I'm not a huge fan of open-plan living, but this was the only open part of the home. The family has three boys under the age of twelve so the parents wanted to have the kitchen open to the great room. The kitchen boasted three islands, which was a challenge to design in a way that did not overwhelm the space. A unique design feature was locating the main working island with the sink and dishwasher in a box bay window looking out to the veranda and pool. I styled this to look like a large piece of furniture floating in front of the window, rather than fitted kitchen cabinetry.

In the great room, I designed a large stone fireplace with a cast limestone mantel and found an antique English carved crest to hang over it. The crest was hand carved in oak and stained dark walnut. The contrast of colors and textures added a rich finishing touch to the fireplace wall. I chose wool, cotton, and leather as textiles to further communicate

A quintessential English gentleman's desk was located
from a dealer in Georgia. The leather top is in a vibrant
green that enhances the citrine color in the paisley
fabric and is a vivid complement to the peacock blue
walls. The combination of colors and finishes creates a
rich and dynamic tableau.

a sense of heritage and warmth that is perennially present in all traditional rooms. I was fortunate to find a monumental-sized Oushak carpet for the entire great room in dark charcoal, tobacco, and blue. This gave the room a noble and well-grounded feeling and created a space that can be used for either formal or informal occasions.

The owners' bedroom wing was patterned after the classical styles of Italian villas; it encompassed the north wing of the house. To create a dramatic entrance, I designed a long, arched colonnade that ran between their bathroom and closets to the sleeping quarters. I selected a blonde wood veneer wallcovering in a parquetry pattern, which created visual interest and gave a modern juxtaposition to the heavy millwork. This impressive path created a forced perspective of the sitting area beyond and helped build a heightened anticipation as one approached the primary sleeping quarters.

A rich and elaborately decorated guest suite was situated next to the primary suite, and I wanted to decorate it using the opposite colors and feel. I selected a dark juniper green for the walls and contrasted the color of walls with light fabrics. A favorite English-style print was chosen for the oversized window treatment and placed on accent pillows on the bedding. A nine-foot-tall poster bed was custom-made and dressed with traditional bed hangings in a true English wool stripe fabric and fan gimp trim. The overall effect was special and perfectly proportioned for the twelve-foot-high ceilings. Proportion was important in a room this large in order to make it feel livable and not too ostentatious.

The south side of the home was where all the service areas were located. A boot room welcomed guests from the side porch, as well as the home-owners, who entered from the garages that flanked the room. The entire service wing of the home was floored in blue slate in a multipiece pattern to resemble bluestone pavers. This made the perfect complement to the printed grass cloth wallcovering in slate blue and ivory. A large expanse of limed oak lockers was designed for both walls of this room in order to keep all the boys' sports and school gear out of sight and to make it easy for them to keep their spaces tidy. For a home as large as this with an active family, this type of storage was a must.

Upstairs was home to the boys' bedrooms, teen lounge, and playroom, all outfitted with durable and hardworking fabrics and furniture. One surprise to all who visit the second floor is a secret "Speakeasy" for Dad and invited guests. This was designed especially for him, so I wanted it to be rich and masculine. I was inspired by the art deco period of the '30s and '40s; this area also showcased a 100-inch flat-screen TV installed above a sleek, serpentine cabinet.

After more than two years of intense planning, construction, and gathering antiques, the house was finally ready to show off to friends and family. Many didn't know what to expect, but the family has been rewarded with flattering compliments from friends and neighbors who undoubtedly will enjoy all the beauty, functionality, and love that exudes from each and every square foot of this special house.

OPPOSITE: Everything in this house had to be special. The lantern in the foyer is from England, the chairs are from Italy, and the rug is antique from Turkey. The front door is custom designed in iron to accompany the formality of the furnishings.

OPPOSITE AND ABOVE: A classic double pedestal dining table with dramatic flame mahogany veneers on the top is surrounded with very stylish scrolling tufted-back chairs in a copper penny iridescent velvet. Host chairs are covered in a muddy green leather. These more masculine and dark colors help convey the Irish manor aesthetic.

ABOVE: A view to the stair hall showcases the detailed millwork in the home. The chair fabric is made for outdoor use so it can take a lot of wear and tear. Greek key nailhead added to the base of the cocktail ottoman gives nice detail.

OPPOSITE: When I went shopping for the living room I told my wife, who assists me on many shopping trips, that I wanted a carved shield or crest with a crown surmounted on top. I walked into a dealer's booth and this cartouche was hanging on the wall. Was it luck or fate?

OPPOSITE: The kitchen has three islands: one for cooking, one for cleaning, and one for eating. Changing the wood finishes and countertops helps the room feel more balanced.

ABOVE: A box bay houses an island with the sink and dishwasher. Two large blue-and-white urn lamps on either end reinforce the look of a large console. Long drapery panels are installed from the ceiling to the floor behind the cabinet, which gives the room the feeling of a living space rather than the utility of a kitchen. This is very intentional as the kitchen is open to the great room and will be seen during social occasions.

RIGHT: The husband wanted a small kitchen dedicated to grilling. This one is right off the grilling porch for easy prep and cleanup.

BELOW: The boot room is an informal entry between garages. This is where the active family can drop book bags, shoes, and coats. The bench in the center of the room is covered in a durable wool plaid.

OPPOSITE: A large hutch in the grilling kitchen is an appropriate spot to display the clients' collection of Woodland Spode dishes. Note the interior window that allows the client to see what's happening in the kitchen and living room while simultaneously prepping for the grill.

ABOVE: Entering the main suite allows a telescoping view down the elegant hall styled after an Italian villa. The forced perspective highlights the pretty and elegant sitting area in the sleeping quarters.

RIGHT: The generously proportioned sleeping quarters feature thirteen-foot ceilings to which I added an overscaled plaster cove molding to help make the room feel smaller and more intimate for sleeping. This room is bathed in neutral tones of cashew and ivory in order to create a serene and quiet look, perfect for relaxing.

OPPOSITE: The suite shows off all the elegant details of the large and opulent room. I tried to imbue a sense of both lightness and softness so the clients would always feel at home here.

ABOVE: The shower echoes the arched window across the room. When designing the shower, I wanted it to have a sense of enclosure, but also allow lots of light. Following the classical scheme for the home, I designed rusticated corners and applied Venetian plaster to give the look and feel of stone.

ABOVE LEFT: Her closet is light and carefree. A French chair is an ideal location to put on shoes or choose the purse of the day.

ABOVE RIGHT: His closet is the yin to her yang. I wanted the closets to be absolutely opposite to each other visually. Walnut for his closet with mirrored doors bounces the natural light from her closet.

OPPOSITE: What a wonderful place to have a bath! An elliptical arch in front of the Palladian-style windows houses the drapery. I love to use sheers in bedrooms and bathrooms because they filter the light and create a romantic effect.

OPPOSITE: This bedroom will leave guests green with envy. The deep green walls are the perfect foil to the light printed window treatment. The bed is a showstopper with a full English-style tester.

ABOVE: The en-suite bathroom complements the green walls with handmade tiles laid in a herringbone pattern. I found the antique brass mirrors (there are a pair in this bathroom) on a shopping trip, and they fit within an inch.

ABOVE: The upstairs hallway is classically styled with wainscoting, chair rail, and fabric-covered walls.

OPPOSITE: The second floor of this home features the children's bedrooms, the children's laundry room, and a media lounge for the children and their friends.

OPPOSITE: The media lounge is covered in a favorite wallcovering that looks like planks of raw cedar. Even when you touch it, the texture fools you. Beyond is the children's terrace.

RIGHT: The terrace off the media lounge is where the children hang out with their friends. This outdoor space is filled with tough-wearing fabrics and furniture. Below is a view of the pool and pavilion.

BELOW: The rear terrace is large and can hold a small group, like this seating for four, or larger groups in other areas of the terrace. I designed the pool pavilion beyond to hide a neighbor's property and to give a terminus to the owners' view.

ABOVE: This end of the large rear terrace is dedicated to lounging and includes a large fireplace and television. The area is easily accessible from the main living area and kitchen.

OPPOSITE: At the other end of the rear terrace are the dining and cooking areas. I like to arrange large living spaces into smaller, intimate spaces so you can feel at home, whether with four people or forty.

MID-ATLANTIC SOLITUDE

ANNAPOLIS, MARYLAND

Vacation homes are always fun to design because clients tend to be more relaxed and less stressed when envisioning a vacation home—this helps them make decisions more easily. In a primary residence, clients spend a lot of emotional energy on selecting the perfect furniture and finishes because they know they will be living with the choices every day. In vacation homes, clients are in residence less frequently, so the choices seem to be easier to make.

For a home in Annapolis, Maryland, the client wanted bright and clean colors. Blue and green seemed the natural choice, since the house sits on the water and has a commanding view of the Chesapeake Bay. But first, she and I had to come to agreement on what shades of green and blue. She astutely pointed out to me that a lot of my work is in muddy, or what I like to call "tea stained," colors. These colors have a smudged quality and give the appearance of patina or that they have aged over time. However, this client did not want an aged appearance. She was very sure of the shades of green and blue she wanted. During the first design direction meeting, I always have the general design scheme laid out for the client to give me feedback. I ask questions such as, "Is this too many patterns in one room for you?" or "Do you like purple for this bedroom?" I ask these questions as I am showing them the fabrics and paint choices I have preselected. This is the clients' chance to offer their input and guide me on what to remove or what they would like to add.

For this waterside home, our first design direction meeting was a little bumpy. The client didn't think I had quite gotten the shade of green she wanted. She said, "Eric, it needs to be Granny Smith apple green." This was very good feedback because I immediately had a reference I could use to make new color and fabric choices. Back to the sample bins I went and shuffled around some of the other fabrics, paints, and wallcoverings.

When my longtime assistant Beth was setting up our conference table and laying out all the selections for our next design meeting, she placed a green apple in the middle of the presentation. I found a small blue-and-white dish to set the apple in so it really made the green pop. We did have to drop a few selections we made previously because they couldn't be reworked with the cleaner color palette. This part of the design process is always bittersweet, because some of our favorite choices can end up on the chopping block. But fearless editing is really the secret to great design.

With our new brighter green and blue color palette, the client was overwhelmingly enthusiastic about her vacation home and ready to start the project as soon as possible. I flew out to Annapolis to get my first look at the home in person and take final measurements. This was in July and she wanted to be in the home by October, so we had to work fast. I quickly brought all the design components together. The main floor was comprised of the great room, dining area, kitchen, and study. All bedrooms were located on the second floor.

I used varying shades of blue throughout the home, in some rooms more than others, in order to create flow and make it easy on the eye to meander out to the sea. As you entered the home, you immediately ascended a short flight of stairs into the great room.

One could see through the rear of the house to the bay. A classic sailboat was moored in the center of the bay, creating a romantic view for this summer house.

The kitchen was charmingly efficient. A classic blue-and-white pattern adorned the back of French-style barstools and was repeated on the Roman shades in the great room. This repetition created continuity and provided rhythm to the spaces as they relate to each other. Simple off-white cabinetry and white subway tile was the perfect foil for the client's very own blue-and-white Chinese export porcelain collection—a personal favorite of mine too! Glass-front cabinets showcased more of the client's collection and allowed her to expand her own dish collections to fill this kitchen.

Because the dining room was attached and open to the great room as well as the kitchen, I wanted to give the client a multiuse space that she could use based on her guests. I sourced an English antique drop leaf table from a dealer in Connecticut and surrounded it with four wicker chairs. The drop leaf table allowed them to push the table against the wall when it's just the client and her husband. They can easily pull out the table and add two more chairs from the living room for additional seating when family comes to visit.

The study was located in the front of the house. We placed a Murphy bed in this room. That way, the client could use this space as a bedroom if more sleeping quarters were needed. But primarily this room functioned as the home office. The walls were covered in a blue basket weave wallcovering with complementary blue-and-white cotton damask window treatments. To create a more masculine feel, I selected a dark stained wood for all of the case goods. I covered the wood floors with a vivid blue-and-green Turkish-patterned area rug.

The home had a small mezzanine level as you go upstairs to the bedrooms. There was a window in the clerestory above the mezzanine, which felt awkward to me. The window was too high to dress with a window treatment and there was a plain, blank wall below it. So, I took the opportunity to place a skirted table on the mezzanine. This acted as a window treatment would have by creating softness for the space. The skirted table also provided a tabletop on which to place decorative objects and a design intermezzo to an otherwise lackluster space.

The top of the stairs provided another stunning view of the sailboat in the harbor beyond as you looked through the double doors to the primary suite. I chose a soft water blue for the walls in this room and added a counterpoint of canary yellow. This classic French color combination worked perfectly for a summer house bedroom. The centerpiece of the room was the commanding four poster bed in dove gray with gold-painted accents. A French toile fabric dressed the windows of the bedroom and walls of the en suite bathroom, as well as the bedding celebrating the client's love of French fabrics and objets d'art.

On the other side of the upper hall were two guest bedrooms. For one guest room, the client and I decided we would use two sets of bunk beds to hold all the grandchildren when they came, and we selected washable bedding in a classic madras plaid. For the other bedroom, we chose more sophisticated bedding for her adult children and other friends who might visit.

This was an important project to me for several reasons. It was my first home on the Chesapeake Bay; it was my first home to decorate in all blue and white; and it was my first home for this special client who is also a friend. We worked so well together and she was so pleased with the results that she asked me to do her primary home in Tennessee. I love repeat clients, especially ones who love color and unique fabrics as much as I do. These working relationships are so rewarding when I get to continue them in other residences. That is always the best compliment.

PRECEDING OVERLEAF: A smart geometric embroidered fabric in varying shades of blue and white covers the thick cushions in the dining room.

OPPOSITE: I love to use lavender colors as an accent in rooms with blue. When I arrived to photograph the house, the homeowner had the same flowers I brought with me to use in this kitchen. I laughed out loud when I saw the flowers.

ABOVE: Who wouldn't love this view? It inspired the colors I used in the home.

OPPOSITE: The entire house is decorated in blue and green with accents of yellow. Of course, we used sailboats and oyster plates as accessories whenever the opportunity arose.

ABOVE: The mezzanine level of the staircase holds a beautiful skirted table topped with blue and white.

ABOVE: This pheasant loves the water views from the owners' bedroom window.

OPPOSITE: When I found the large print of the swan with the yellow lotus in the water, I had to have it for this room! It is splendid over the bed. The effect of all of the design choices in the bedroom suite are calming but also dramatic.

OPPOSITE: I love to mix finishes of wood furniture because it gives a more collected look, as if the room were curated over time and from many sources. I applied several of my tried-and-true design tricks in this room: a combination of fabrics on upholstery, ceramic stools for tables, and waterfowl art.

ABOVE: The wallpaper adds a jovial feeling in bright aqua and the yellow evokes the warmth of sunshine. A stool is great to have by a tub to easily reach towels or a robe after bathing.

ABOVE: This corner of the study gives a small view into the bathroom.

OPPOSITE: Here the desk is placed in front of the window to take advantage of the woodland view. A blue-and-green Turkish rug adds a lively element.

RIGHT: The en-suite bathroom has a bold blue-and-white ikat printed stripe wallcovering to complete the look. In small bathrooms, a bolder wallcovering is necessary to create more visual interest and energy. This paper shows the profound effect wallcovering can have on otherwise ordinary spaces.

BELOW AND OPPOSITE: I found a playful chinoiserie print in blue and green on a white background and painted the walls a bright French hydrangea blue in this room.

OPPOSITE: Custom embroidered bedding gives bold contrast to the happy chinoiserie print in this guest bedroom. The apple green check bench is a great spot for guest's luggage. I like to use benches or stools in guest rooms rather than a luggage rack because they are multifunctional.

LONE STAR SHOWCASE

FORT WORTH, TEXAS

I love Texas. I was born and raised in Kentucky and have lived in Tennessee now for more than thirty years, but I spent four of the best years of my life at Baylor University in Waco, Texas. I spent those very formative years with amazing people, delicious food, and flat plains where you can see forever. It is always fun to return to the Lone Star State and be reminded of why it continues to draw people to live there. So, when I was asked to decorate a home in Fort Worth, I jumped at the chance to work with some of my favorite Texans.

The relationship started like many of mine do, by a referral from a former client. I had done work for the client's sister, and because she had thoroughly vetted me and sold me as a designer, the new clients were ready to begin the design process with me right away.

With out-of-town projects, I always begin the research process through a FaceTime interview where the clients can show me around the house and explain to me their pain points and where they need solutions. For this project, the couple had recently finished a major renovation of the home and now had a more open floor plan. Their main concern was that they didn't have enough seating in their living room and needed help creating a space that connected well to the open kitchen and outdoor living spaces. They didn't know how to place their furniture in this new open plan.

In my experience, most people do not have enough seating in their living rooms. If you have to move folding chairs into your spaces for gatherings, you simply do not have enough seats in your rooms.

A good rule of thumb to make sure you have enough seating in your house is to have as many seats in the living spaces as your home can sleep. So, if your home sleeps ten, you should be able to seat ten in the living room. If your home sleeps eight, you should be able to seat eight. (Don't use bunks or bunk rooms in this tabulation, as they are more for overflow guests.)

Once I had the major design points noted, I booked my travel plans and went on the site visit to get measurements and a full inventory of the furniture that was going to remain in the new design. The client had several wonderful family heirlooms, as his father had been in the retail furniture business and collected some great pieces: a beautiful buffet to reuse in the dining room, a charming tall case clock, and some interesting stone lamps. After noting all the items to reuse, I got to work creating floor plans for the spaces we all agreed needed to be redesigned.

The home had a very simple entry hall that was quite small, but I wanted to make it more visually interesting to create the look of a proper foyer. To that end, I found a lovely flora-and-fauna motif wallcovering in cremes and grays with touches of peacock blue and terra-cotta, from which I pulled colors for the rest of the house.

The entry hall opened immediately into the large formal dining room, which we covered in a gravel-colored grass cloth. The moody and sludgy gray tone of the wallcovering was a pretty counterpoint to the amount of daylight that poured in through a large box bay window. I recovered their dining chairs in a peacock blue epingle velvet set atop a cream-colored modern lattice-patterned area rug. The contrast in tones really made the dark dining table and chairs pop. Finally, I designed a small custom bench covered in an iridescent velvet to tuck into the box bay widow and flanked it with the clients' antique Japanese hand-painted urns. They requested we put these in a place of honor—this was the perfect location highlighting their colors and grand scale.

The new open floor plan of the home now adjoined the dining room, great room, and kitchen. Previously, the great room furniture was arranged much too closely. To help remedy this, I placed a large Turkish-style area rug in the room, which allowed me to pull the seating arrangement farther apart and accommodate more seating areas. This new seating arrangement also allowed the furniture to align with the new large sliding door and window unit that opened onto the covered outdoor living area.

In most of the homes I design, I take the opportunity to decorate primary bedrooms in completely different color schemes from the other rooms. I like to use the opportunity as a departure from the main house color palette and really do something quite the opposite. For this project, I selected a bright French hydrangea blue for the walls paired with fabrics in shades of ivory. The blue is vivid, so the ivory serves to create a more tranquil environment for rest and relaxation. I continued the ivory palette in the en suite bathroom with a cream-and-linen striped wallcovering. This color scheme really allowed the existing marble floors and shower to shine in the complementary ivory color.

Returning to Texas to create a beautiful and well-appointed home was a cherished treat. Out-of-town projects can be challenging due to logistical issues that arise, but the challenges are worth the effort. This project remains special, not only because the rooms finished so beautifully, but also for new friendships formed with the clients. They were so appreciative of the better flow and function of rooms, and most pleased that I found ways to include their cherished family heirlooms. These heirlooms now shine in the new redesign and are reminders of a rich family history.

OPPOSITE: The collection of exotic bird prints are a reproduction of an antique textile and enhance all of the colors in the living room. An antique beaded sari adds interest to the tight back sofa.

The seating inside the home has a great relationship with the outdoor seating area. In pleasant weather, the doors can stay open and guests both indoors and out can associate easily with each other.

Designing History Michael S. Smith

BRITISH DESIGNERS AT HOME JENNY ROSE-INNES

AUDUBON'S ANIMALS JOHN JAMES AUDUBON
The Viviparous Quadrupeds
of North America

RIGHT: A custom settee is covered in cerulean blue velvet and topped with an embroidered silk lampas pillow in colors of Imari. The color scheme echoes the clients' monumental Japanese vases that live in the box bay of the dining room.

BELOW: In this foyer, the wallpaper showcases birds in terra-cotta and blue, setting the color scheme for the entire house. A brass lamp with birds on a branch continues the avian theme.

OPPOSITE: The dining table and chairs are a cherished set the clients have enjoyed for many years. They love to entertain so the table is set with all the leaves so a large group can be hosted at a moment's notice.

ABOVE: A small café table sits in a bay window off the kitchen with views of the rear of the property. The client found the table and I added the antique French chairs in a chippy paint finish for contrast.

OPPOSITE: The living room is quite neutral with a hand-printed chintz applied to chairs the clients used previously. I love repurposing clients' things when designing new rooms to provide emotional comfort and history.

OPPOSITE: The quintessential antique French lounge chairs in blue sateen match the wall color perfectly and create a small sitting area at the foot of the bed.

ABOVE: The owners' en-suite bath was already remodeled with ivory and gold marble when I arrived. All it needed was a soft neutral wallcovering to give the room more visual interest and personality. Wallcovering is a must in every bathroom I decorate.

URBAN RESTRAINT

DOWNTOWN NASHVILLE, TENNESSEE

I have been decorating houses professionally for more than twenty-five years now. When I began my career, I designed and decorated houses in various styles. Being in the South, I did a majority of my work in the traditional style and, because I was just starting out, I had to bend to the taste and style of whoever called. I was eager to please all types of clients and in all types of projects because I needed to gain experience and, let's face it, make a living. As I matured professionally, I have been able to fine-tune my client list and say no to projects that don't fit my design style—Southern traditional. So, when a prospective client called to ask me to do their new modern-style house in downtown Nashville, I was hesitant to say yes.

If you asked me to give an example of the opposite of my typical design project, this home would be it. But I was intrigued by the opportunity to work on what I call a "tall and skinny" house. These are new homes that have been built on what were previously single home lots, now subdivided to accommodate two homes. This new infill development category is happening all over the country in older, more established neighborhoods. It is controversial due to the size and shape (tall and skinny) and how they are crowding the landscape in many urban cores. What attracted me to this project, though, was not that it would challenge my design preferences. It was about the clients who were asking me to work for them. The wife explained that she followed me on social media and knew our styles did not necessarily match, but that she loved the way I worked on projects. She had been

watching me on the weekly series I was posting online called "Today in the Studio" and really liked how straightforward my design process was. She asked me to consider working with her and her husband on their new house.

Our first meeting, as with most of my in-town projects, was in the home. I was impressed with the quality of finishes as well as the design of the living areas, which were vast and had large windows that created a wonderful quality of light. Of course, I was also charmed by the delightful young couple. They were very eager to hear what I thought of the home and if I could imagine an interior they described as "warm modern." After our hour together, I was excited to see what we could create as a team.

This home, for all its modernity, was a split-level house. As a child of the '70s, I am very familiar with this style of home because I grew up in one. In my opinion, the entry of a split-level home is the least impressive entry you can have, because it's not a room, but rather a stairway. As you enter, you have to go either up or down, so you don't have the ability to create a mood with such design devices as furniture or accessories. There was also a large expanse of drywall and glass, which I felt needed to be warmed up and given scale so visitors would feel comfortable upon entering. Humans crave scale, which is the ability to feel as if they "fit" in a space. If a space is too large and staggering, people tend to feel uneasy and try to leave quickly. To counter this overwhelming feeling, I found two monumental-sized modern art pieces on canvas. A small urn on stand with artfully arranged branches was placed in the corner by the door to give an organic foil to the starkness of the space.

At the top of the staircase, I placed a small hall table with a lamp and velvet chair with a woven dragon design to greet visitors. I find that Asian motifs fit well in modern architecture. Asian art is so fanciful and full of symbolism, which can counter the coldness of modern rooms. Beyond this landing lay more large, open-plan rooms—the kitchen, dining room, and living area, all on full display. I designed these spaces to be perceived as separated in use but connected by color. To that end, I chose blue and white, a personal favorite, as the color palette for these public spaces.

The living room had a large wall of plate glass windows that allowed in most of the natural light on this floor of the home. I decided to hang drapery panels along just one side of the window in an asymmetric style rather than installing them in the more traditional pair of panels hanging on opposite sides of the window. To balance the wide single drapery panel, I selected an oversized brass floor lamp. It had an industrial look but was crafted in unlacquered brass, which helped give a warm feeling. A large, bold, striped area rug in ink blue and gray anchored the large sitting area. Atop the rug, the sofa was arranged on one side across from two tobacco brown leather chairs with exposed wood frames.

An ample-sized daybed covered in gray chenille stands in front of the concrete tile slab-style fireplace. The fabric of the daybed warms up the frigid materials of the fireplace as well as invites the user to come, sit, and enjoy the fire.

Flanking the fireplace are a pair of Japanese-style, blue-and-white porcelain urns on Venetian plastered plinths. These hide the unfortunate view of the old house next door and create symmetry to give a well-balanced look to the room.

The open floor plan gave little separation of the living room, dining room, and kitchen. In order to create visual separation, I chose a leopard print rug in similar colors and tones to the living room rug. The dining room table had a whitewashed oak finish; I surrounded the table with barrel-style side chairs upholstered in a combination of fabrics. With limited areas to use fabrics, I chose two for the dining chairs—a woven chenille for the inside of the chairs and a stylized cherry-blossom motif fabric for the outside of the chairs. I arranged coordinating barstools at the kitchen island to use for overflow seating for guests or as a more intimate dining spot for the homeowners.

Upstairs the home had two bedrooms on either side of a small loft with an attached wet bar. For this loft space, there was no natural light in the room. When a room is naturally dark, many times I find it more effective to just go with dark colors, rather than try to lighten it up. People will always struggle to get a sense of light in naturally dark spaces, so I find darker colors just feel more well suited. I covered the wall in a dark navy wallcovering featuring concentric circles of silver. The silver can shimmer when the lights are on. This helped bounce the light around the room. I designed a large sectional in cocoa brown fabric for one side of the room and a desk on the other, which the homeowners could use as a home office. A bold cobalt blue velvet ottoman in the center of the room served as a counterpoint to the darkness of the other finishes.

The primary bedroom was on the brighter side of the house. I chose to drape the entire south wall with window treatments and placed a large, modern bookcase crafted in wood and metal in front of the drapes. The softness of the drapery and the hardness of the bookcase created an interesting play of masculine and feminine in this space.

My favorite rooms to design are bedrooms, and I always design them with a more feminine bent than masculine, with lots of fabrics and frills. Of course, this can be a challenge in a modern space. The entire primary bedroom was designed in shades of gray, but I selected the upholstery carefully to give a feminine touch. The upholstered bed was selected for its soft corners and pretty nailhead details. I also chose a curved and feminine silhouette for the small sofa at the foot of the bed. Other nods to femininity were the hand-painted bureau in water tones and using lavender as the only other accent color in the room. The overall effect was warm and soft as I think bedrooms should be.

The small guest room was designed using all neutrals, leaning toward beige and cream tones rather than gray. The bed, upholstered in a silver sage chenille, was placed across from the large expanse of glass windows and in front of a bold ikat fabric wallcovering. The energy from the movement of the wallcovering balanced the energy coming from the city skyline views. A small bench in a modern epingle velvet provided a perch for guests to sit on while they put on shoes or to place an overnight bag.

What a happy outcome we all had with this project! The clients were extremely happy with the results of the design and how I softened their more modern leanings. I was surprised at how I could use my Southern traditional design voice in a more modern home. This collaboration of different design styles and aesthetic predispositions was a great lesson in learning for both of us, and the pleasing result speaks for itself.

OPPOSITE: Split levels are difficult to decorate due to the lack of floor space. Here I use scale as a decorating device. The art packs a punch and fills the volume of space.

A singular urn with branches creates a natural element to contrast with the rigidity of the modern stair rail.

ABOVE: The dining room's built-in server is topped with a large Norfolk pine in a Chinese export porcelain planter, giving the feeling of a bonsai without the maintenance.

OPPOSITE: The modern kitchen was existing when I began the project. I added the pendant lights to give a jewel-like appearance and warm up an otherwise cold interior space.

OPPOSITE: The upstairs loft has no natural light, so rather than fighting against the darkness of the space, I embraced it with dark charcoal wallcovering. A sectional sofa is tucked in the corner for napping or watching TV.

ABOVE: The wallcovering in the loft has a great effect on the space with its reflective foil ink. It bounces what little light comes into the room and provides visual interest.

OPPOSITE: The main suite has loose art deco motifs on the upholstered bed and settee. Art deco in modern homes provides a nice provenance to the past.

ABOVE: The draped wall provides the ideal foil against an extremely modern étagère. The French antique chair is a wonderful contrast to the modern furniture in this room, but still feels relevant among the modern touches.

OPPOSITE: The owners' en-suite bath has floating white birch cabinetry and white tile. To create more character, I chose a classic Scalamandré wallcovering in gray tones.

RIGHT: A modern bathroom can feel sterile, but a well-placed chair gives softness and comfort to a utilitarian space.

BELOW: The guest bedroom has adjacent views of a park—a delight in a city house—so I placed the bed opposite the windows to take advantage of the view. A paper-backed ikat silk fabric on the walls echoes the sense of rhythm and energy of the city and speaks to the modernity of city living.

AMONG THE LIVE OAKS

COLUMBIA, SOUTH CAROLINA

Columbia, South Carolina, is a quintessential Southern town with history and charm on every corner. The state capitol—and home to the South Carolina Gamecocks—its citizens are well educated and well-heeled. I was fortunate to attract one of its native residents who had returned home to retire with his wife, who was a follower of mine on social media. She messaged me to ask if I would be interested in decorating their historic home. Of course, I jumped at the chance to imbue my Southern traditional aesthetic on a grande dame in one of the oldest sections of town.

The two-story Craftsman home was set on a corner lot with majestic live oaks and one of the oldest deodar cedars in the state. The house was painted in an all-white exterior, which works well on a heavily shaded lot as it sparkles in the dappled sunlight. The main floor was almost entirely empty—the clients wanted to redesign the rooms with all new furniture, draperies, rugs, and art. This was a dream project that let me start from scratch in almost every room, and the clients encouraged me to let my creativity go in whatever direction it chose. The clients had been following me on social media for several months and trusted from my other projects that they would love my efforts.

For the foyer, they already owned a large framed de Gournay wallcovering panel. It was quite dramatic with a gold leaf background, so I chose a yellow Ousak-style carpet and sat a silk brocade skirted table in the center of the room. I love skirted tables and am always looking for occasions to incorporate them into my designs. The foyer was almost square so the round skirted table was the perfect shape for the room and warmly welcomed guests as they entered the historic home.

The living room was one of the main reasons the clients loved the house. It was a sizable room, and they wanted to be able to host large gatherings with ample seating. I pride myself on being able to get a lot of seats in a room, so I gladly took on the challenge. I created a seating plan that was more of a lounge feel than a formal living room. Sofas and chairs were arranged in different parts of the room to encourage conversation in the different spaces rather than all around one central area. If they host a smaller group, people can congregate in one of the seating areas, and if they host a larger gathering, then guests can find various seating arrangements, some more intimate and some more sizable.

The dining room extended directly off the living room, which allowed for great traffic flow during celebrations and holiday entertaining. The clients had an antique buffet and mirror that they wanted to use in the dining room. I decided to use a slightly murky wall color and texture, so I chose a fog-colored grass cloth for the walls and a pale aloe green fabric for the window treatments. I like moody dining rooms, because they look great by candlelight. I contrasted the dining chairs in a pretty chenille stripe with beige, brown, and green with the host chairs in an embroidered matelassé. I love the texture a matelassé brings to a project and by over-embroidering the quilted fabric, the chairs have a sophisticated charm that is perfect for the dining room in this old, historic home.

The family room was located at the rear of the house and was most certainly a later addition to the original structure. This room was a large, single story and had a beamed ceiling and six-inch grooved wall paneling. A fireplace at one end grounded the room and balanced the open kitchen on the opposite end. For the sofa, I chose a brown-and-white houndstooth fabric with pillows in an epingle ikat and flora-and -fauna print. I upholstered chairs on one end of the room in a rich tobacco with Chippendale-inspired band trim at the skirt.

Living in and decorating a historic home takes someone who truly loves history and old things and understands how to live with them. There are so many idiosyncrasies in old houses that need to be appreciated. From the age and quality of the building materials to the difficulty of plaster walls and ceilings, a historic home is not for the faint of heart. By deftly combining new with the old, this 100-year-old house now feels relevant, but also preserved in a world where so many old homes are destroyed to make way for the new. Sharing this thoughtfully designed and curated home with others will be one of the many joys the homeowners will have for years to come.

RIGHT: The skirted table in the foyer displays a small antique pocket watch that belonged to the client's grandfather. The fabric is silk lampas.

OPPOSITE: A de Gournay hand-painted wall panel was in the foyer when I began the project. I didn't want anything to distract from its appeal, so I kept all fabrics and finishes neutral throughout the formal rooms of the house.

OVERLEAF: A large rug grounds the various seating arrangements. The color palette is very simple with pale blues and grays in furnishings and window treatments. This allows for the focus to be on the historic architecture in the room.

ABOVE: The formal living has multiple seating areas for guests. This side of the large room shows off the scalloped sofa and the clients' armchair recovered in a cut velvet.

OPPOSITE: Small areas of interest in a room can surprise and delight family and guests. I spend hours accessorizing and refining the placement of every item I use in a home, especially if they are personal treasures the client brings to the project.

OPPOSITE: Antiques are so important! Here the server, mirror, and tea service were already in the clients' collection. I added the table and chairs to complement every piece the clients owned.

ABOVE: Light is such an important element in design. The silk window treatments in the dining room have an iridescent quality, especially in early evening as seen in this photo.

This kitchen is situated in the middle of the house, a rarity in older homes, which truly makes it the heart of this home.

OPPOSITE: A small, round table sits by the fireplace for intimate dinners when the homeowners are at home alone or for lunch with a friend. The table is flanked with two modern-style wing chairs in a fresh blue, green, and white stripe. Tucked under the table is a whimsical hoofed-foot ottoman to be used either as a footstool or another seat.

ABOVE: South Carolina is known for its Lowcountry marshlands. Even though this home is in the Midlands, the painting over the sofa feels perfectly placed in the den, echoing the blues and greens used in the fabrics of this room.

COLONIAL ALLURE

COLLEGE GROVE, TENNESSEE

The clients for this project found me by attending an open house in their neighborhood. I had designed and decorated a large house three years earlier, and it was now on the market. By some miracle, the realtor did not strip all the wallpaper and paint it white, as is the norm today. So the house appeared as it had when I finished it—full of wallpaper and color. The neighbors walked through and fell in love with it; they were considered placing an offer. But, as they discussed it, they decided that they didn't need a larger house, they just needed their current house to be decorated like this one. That's when I got the call from them to come and infuse their current house with Southern style and charm.

The house was efficiently laid out with a center hall flanked by a study on the left and the dining room on the right. I love a center hall in a home as it creates a strong central axis to guide visitors through the spine of the house, making travel from one end to the other easy. The center staircase can also become a strong architectural design feature if you dress it properly. In this case, I chose an antelope print carpet as a runner, which created an interesting pattern with a lot of motion and character. There was not a lot of room for furniture in the center hall—it demanded a wallcovering to create more visual interest instead.

The clients owned almost all of the furniture they needed, but it was still necessary for me to add my special combination of decor and details in order to make the home welcoming and gracious. They had a glass-front hutch in the dining room that was too large and a small table in the sitting room with a tall mirror over it that felt too small where it was. I swapped the table and mirror in the sitting room with the oversized hutch in the dining room and voila! The rooms were suddenly balanced and the pieces looked at home.

The dining room had existing wainscoting installed on the lower sixty inches of the wall. To give a more robust mood in the room, I selected a printed grass cloth featuring a dense tree line in tones of sage, olive, and tan. The woven paper and the saturation of pattern and color gave the appearance of tapestry fabric, rather than a wallcovering, contributing a richer feeling to the room.

One architectural issue in the dining room was limited windows. There was only a single window in the room, so the window treatment needed to have presence. To that end, I designed an elaborate window treatment in a style called *en tableau*. It is akin to a stage curtain where the panels are drawn up on the diagonal, which brings the stack of the curtain higher, allowing more natural light in the room.

Across the hall was the sitting room. It had the same high wainscoting detail on the walls that was in the dining room, so I contrasted the ample use of white on the trim with one of my favorite dark coral paint colors for the walls above. I chose a soft teal linen print for the window treatments complemented by a wool sheer with a pinstripe to help diffuse the strong sunlight that came into that room. New slipcovers were made for existing side chairs in a coral chenille. I fashioned buttons up the back of the chairs to give them a dressmaker detail, easily seen from the foyer. Stylish details like that add a lot of charm to a room.

Just beyond the rear of the central hallway, the great room opened up to a large kitchen and breakfast room. The great room had margin for more seating than the clients had been using. We decided to start from scratch on the furnishings. A pair of sofas lived on each end of the room with the fireplace in the center. If you have followed my work for any period of time, you will know my love of pairs is a constant and I have used them here to great effect. Handsome paisley and stripe window treatments in blue, cream, and terra-cotta pull the colors together to finish the design scheme of the room.

The kitchen and breakfast room fabrics coordinated beautifully with the blues, terra-cotta, and cremes I showcased in the great room. The clients already had a lovely antique French table and chair set. I designed new chair cushions and window treatments and added a small, patterned rug for under the table to warm up this area. They needed more storage in this room to hold linens, tableware, and a collection of blue-and-white Chinese export porcelain. The solution: a large console with open shelving in a distressed white, which helped draw in the color of the kitchen cabinetry and acted as a contrast to the dark wood of the table and chairs. This created a pleasing dynamic between the two areas of the room.

My main goal in bedrooms is to always make them relaxing. By continuing the same print on the bedding and windows in this bedroom suite, I created a restful mood in the room, rather than using multiple types of prints and patterns, which could have been visually disruptive. For the upholstery, I chose a beige velvet for the sofa and added a similar colored Oriental teahouse woven fabric for pillows and skirted ottomans at the foot of the bed. My favorite find for this room was the gold leaf Swedish clock from a local antique store. The size, color, and silhouette felt perfectly at home in this bedroom.

What started as an unconventional way to get a new client ended as a favorite project. These clients are definitely some of my most cherished because they trusted me completely. After all, they had almost bought an entirely new house just because they loved the decorating! When they had me decorate their house, there was no questioning or hedging my decisions. They allowed me to create a similar alluring design in their home, and their faith in me shines through in the beautiful outcome of the project.

OPPOSITE: Is there anything more English than a tall case clock? This one feels at home in this foyer surrounded by a favorite hydrangea vine wallcovering. I chose the antelope runner for the stairs to imbue a touch of whimsy to the reserved room.

PRECEDING OVERLEAF: Dining chairs in an epingle velvet stripe perfectly match the neutral shades of green and cream in the Oushak-style rug.

ABOVE: Natural light is always the best asset to any room. The *en tableau* window treatment makes the dining room feel proper and elegant while allowing more light into the room.

OPPOSITE: A gold swan lamp on a tall English chest adds contrast to the high wainscoting in the dining room.

PRECEDING OVERLEAF: A pair of cocktail ottomans in front of the sofas, a pair of French reproduction fauteuils with a heavy epingle tapestry flanking the fireplace, and a pair of swivel club chairs across the room round out the generous seating area and attest to my love of pairs in creating effective and satisfying designs.

OPPOSITE: The breakfast room is a cheerful space to start the day.

RIGHT: Fruit in a kitchen is always a good idea—here a favorite series of gourd prints enhance the open shelf server in the breakfast room.

BELOW: Swivel chairs act as a room divider in this open floor plan design scheme. Guests can participate with ease in conversations in the great room, breakfast room, or kitchen.

ABOVE: A favorite lamp sits atop a chest with a traditional set of botanicals above. Chinoiserie is a preferred motif of mine and the female figure here completes the pretty tableau.

OPPOSITE: A soft gray-blue covers the walls accompanied by a simple, but fanciful blue-and-cream print on the bedding and window treatments. I love blue and, at this point in my career, it's not a secret.

A curved, pleated valance treatment hangs from decorative wooden rods over traversing draperies. These window treatments incorporate an elaborate style to balance the whimsy of the canopy bed.

CREATING ELAN

FRANKLIN, TENNESSEE

The South is full of beautiful plantation-style homes, old and new. Some are more formal and traditionally styled with double-height columns supporting roofs for shaded loggias and some are a more vernacular style featuring deep, charming porches with wicker and large ferns and prolific flowers. Both are a welcome sight as one drives through various neighborhoods of estates lined with trees and fences delineating properties large and small. It's difficult to choose a favorite because they both hearken to times past, which make them so desirable to many Southerners. For a young couple who had been on the lookout for a new place, one of these homes called to them and presented an opportunity to create something exciting from a tired, old grande dame.

This project came up when good friends reached out to me to ask if I would look at a house they were considering for purchase. They thought it had great curb appeal and good bones, but it needed what they described as "superficial changes." I took a quick look at the potential property online and called them back to give my feedback. The house was situated in the country with several acres. It had a lovely horse fence surrounding the property and a pool. The style of the home was Louisiana plantation with double porches across the front and a romantic façade to the street. However, that was where the charm ended. Inside the house was circa 1990 with a few updates in the early aughts that caused the interiors to look like a poor version of old-world Europe. I suggested we expand the scope of work to include redoing almost the entire first floor.

The main issue with the house was the layout; it was not made for modern living and entertaining. The first floor living spaces were a maze of hallways and small doorways. The kitchen was separated from the public areas. A large den at the far rear of the main floor was a complete dead end; you couldn't get anywhere once you entered the den. Nothing flowed. For today's lifestyle, homeowners want rooms that lead from one into the next. This makes the house more instinctual for guests to use without having to be guided through the spaces.

To rework this clumsy type of layout, many architects create a central spine or axis that allows people to easily get across a home through an open hallway or a series of rooms where one leads into another. This creates better traffic flow for entertaining and also allows sight lines so you can see from one room to the next. It also gives a larger sense of space and allows the rooms to share window exposure, bringing in more natural light. To that end, I significantly widened cased openings between the dining room and formal living room. I also opened a pair of doorways flanking the living room fireplace. A previous guest room became the den, and I moved the guest room to the rear of the main floor where the den had been. Now guests staying overnight would have more privacy than they would have situated off the living room.

Of course, new finishes were required throughout the home. The clients requested every room be light and bright. The kitchen was completely gutted, and all new white cabinets and professional appliances were chosen. I significantly expanded the window

OPPOSITE: Large paneled wainscoting in the living room adds to an elegant and bright room. The large painting continues the color scheme of navy and mint used for the rooms throughout the house.

ABOVE: Many people call lamps and decorative lighting the jewelry of a home. I like to buy the best so they last the longest. In this otherwise neutral room, a Ming-style lamp in mint adds both contrast and interest.

OVERLEAF: With the addition of the butler's pantry, the dining room becomes more of a square shape. When I have a square dining room in a project, I always use a round dining table. We repeated the round shape of the table with a round-shaped tray ceiling detail. This adds a surprising and stunning detail.

OPPOSITE: We completely disassembled the existing kitchen and made way for this dream kitchen. A taller and wider window was added over the kitchen sink. The mosaic marble on the backsplash in the kitchen is repeated on the floor of the butler's pantry.

ABOVE: The butler's pantry is cleverly hidden by mirror front doors in a wall of glass display cabinetry. As the doors open, one is delighted by marble mosaic floors and more mirrored front millwork that hides ample storage for food and beverages. The room is open at the end with an ice maker and beverage fridge that can act as a bar off the attached sunroom.

175

over the sink in order to feature a view of the hills beyond the property. A decadent butler's pantry was made from a large closet off the rear hallway.

The original home featured a beautiful sweeping staircase in the foyer, which we kept. I added panelized walls painted in a soft shade of white. I also added arches to the new, enlarged cased openings, as well as the small anteroom that leads between the foyer and rear hallway. On one side of the foyer is the dining room, which connects to the new kitchen. Navy grass cloth was selected for the walls, and gold accents create a dynamic contrast in a room that will mostly be used in the evenings with candlelight.

Across the foyer from the dining room was the living room. As in the rest of the house, the addition of significant millwork and architectural details elevated the blandness of the interiors and injected more stature and elegant appeal. I kept the fabrics light, but repeated the navy from the dining room with a novelty print on the tailored window treatments.

On either side of the newly styled living room fireplace were deep alcove passageways that led to the relocated study. I added more millwork to the walls and painted all of it a palomino beige color. Dark navy velvet and rich cognac leather infused the home with a masculine touch. By opening this room to the living room and using it as a study, now all of the public rooms were along the front of the house.

Upstairs the home boasted a healthy four bedrooms. To make this space more usable, the clients requested we add a rear staircase. The existing floor plan had a side entry that allowed access to a small

lagoon. I thought this would be the perfect location for the staircase, which would allow the side entry to look and function like a secondary foyer. We did have to lose a full bathroom with this choice, but we were able to replace it with a half bath tucked under the new stairs.

For outdoor living, the clients wanted to add a large, covered porch off the pool for parties. We created a porch and outdoor fireplace. Instead of roofing the structure, we were able to use the porch roof as an open deck for sunbathing off the bedrooms on the second floor. The new sundeck also allows lovely views of the pool and property for guests when they stay overnight.

Lastly, we painted the entire house three shades of white and cream with a soft green shutter. When I showed the new shutter color to the client, she demurred saying she really didn't like green. I asked her to trust me and try it on the front of the house and we could change it. We both agreed it was perfect when the house was finished.

Could we have possibly made more changes to this house to make it more exceptional? I think not. The dramatic outcome of this project showed what can be accomplished when you think outside the box and are ruthless with taking down walls and turning a house on its head by reimagining room locations and functions. I love remodeling projects where I can really take a diamond in the rough and polish it until it shines. This one is uniquely special. Not just because the clients are beloved friends, but because they trusted me to bring my vision to fruition. What a thrill to see the results.

OPPOSITE: Black bamboo Chinese Chippendale chairs add heft and drama to the casual room. They repeat the color from the black iron on the console in the foreground.

RIGHT: In this room, a former guest bedroom before the renovation, I added window treatments, molding, and paint, and recovered this chair in a chenille stripe. The wood cocktail table was formerly on a covered porch. I love to rearrange furniture—knowing how to adequately arrange furniture to make a room usable and inviting is a special skill.

BELOW: Decorative pillows are so important in rooms. They create texture and depth as well as comfort when taking a nap or lumbar support when sitting.

OPPOSITE: The bay window overlooks a pond on the property. Many of my clients live in pastoral settings, and maximizing the views to the outdoors always adds to the beauty of the homes.

OPPOSITE: The sunroom is directly between the kitchen and covered porch. A daybed in front of the window allows for views both out to the pool and in to the kitchen.

ABOVE: A rear set of stairs is placed where a bathroom used to be located. We maintained the bathroom by tucking it under the stairs.

OPPOSITE: A guest bedroom was moved from the front of the house to the rear to improve the flow of the public rooms needed for entertaining. The change also gives the house a much larger guest bedroom on the main floor for aging parents.

ABOVE: I like to put desks in bedrooms when possible. The clients' collection of luggage is a handsome addition to this space.

ABOVE AND OPPOSITE: The bathrooms feature light marble tiles and
counters. In the primary bath, an arched opening between his and her
vanities showcases a new tub and shower area with a large window.
I love to use sparkly finishes in bathrooms, and the mosaic marble
floors in this bathroom create a glittering effect.

BRIGHT ON THE WATER

GRAND RIVERS, KENTUCKY

Over the years, many of my clients have allowed me to design and decorate not just their main residences, but also their vacation homes. More often than not, clients aren't as finicky about a vacation home reflecting their personal style as they would be in their main home. In fact, most clients want their second or third residences to be a complete departure from their normal style so it feels like a retreat or diversion from their ordinary existence.

This is what I recently did at a home for my niece and her family in western Kentucky. Situated in a private enclave tucked around a small inlet off the main channel of Kentucky Lake, was her Craftsman cottage vacation home. I have worked on multiple projects with my niece and her husband, who is a residential and commercial builder in the area. At this point, we have a very symbiotic relationship from working together closely on so many projects.

My niece and I both love blue, and it felt like a natural choice for the home given its proximity to the water. Blue and green together has perennially been my favorite color scheme, so we settled on this color palette throughout the house. In secondary residences, I like to keep the design schemes very consistent and concise among the various spaces. This creates a more calming effect in a home where rest and relaxation is the goal.

The lot sloped dramatically toward the water's edge, and the house was large even though it was cottage style. We chose a house plan that would hide half of the home's square footage in the lower level, giving the street view a one and a half story appearance. The massing of the structure from the

street was important due to the proximity to other houses on the street. The exterior of the house was almost entirely clad in a mix of gray and beige stone with white mortar. I love using white mortar on stone houses as it creates a fresher appearance than gray or beige. We chose to paint the small amount of accent shingle shake siding in a bright aqua to communicate a cheery, summertime appearance since the home will be used the most in summer.

Upon entering the two-story foyer, you are drawn to the view through the great room out to the water, beckoning visitors to discover what is beyond. A vintage model of a sailboat placed on the console in the living room behind the sofa functioned as a divider between foyer and great room. The great room was crowned with large cedar beams and illuminated with ample windows to bring in the natural light and, of course, the water's edge. This room's layout allowed for ample seating for ten. The great room shared easy access to the breakfast area and large kitchen with keeping room. The open nature of the room arrangements allowed for hosting a great crowd of friends and family for holidays or long weekends.

To the left of the foyer was a large octagon-shaped dining room. I wanted this room to be eclectic, relaxed, and elegant. I chose a large-scale Jacobean wallcovering for the upper story of the fourteen-foot-ceiling room. I fell in love with a blue-and-green chinoiserie-inspired toile for the window treatments. Many of my design devotees over the years love how I mix and match many different patterns together, and I admit this is one of my favorite mixes: toile and florals.

OPPOSITE: Blue chenille for the sofas and a printed stripe for chairs brings a peaceful mood to the room. A large leather-topped coffee table invites guests to put their feet up and relax.

A large, dark wood dining table contrasted well with the white panelized walls. I surrounded the table with woven chairs and loose striped seat cushions for a relaxed appearance. The real showstopper in this room was the daring use of black-and-gold leopard print on the rug, bordered in bright blue for a playful contrast of what could be seen as a dressy choice for the floor. The combination of all of these finishes brought an enchanting feeling to the space, which is ideal for a vacation home dining room.

Across the hall from the dining room was the home office. I wanted this to be an area that could be used for light work when someone needed a little privacy to answer emails or call clients if necessary. Because this is a second home, there was no need for a full-blown office space, so I chose a small writing desk with armchairs and a matching bookcase. The wallcovering in this space showcased silhouettes of citrine-colored trees on a peacock blue sisal ground, continuing the blue-and-green scheme of the home. A large and colorful Oushak-style area rug finished the spirited color palette.

For the kitchen, my only parameter to work within was blue cabinets. My niece had been hesitant in suggesting the cabinet color thinking I would not like the idea, but I loved it. We selected a pale blue that would be easy to live with in the long term. I found an exuberant mosaic backsplash that reminded me of an old quilting pattern. It was a marble hexagon design, which I suspect was intended to be modern, but I liked the folksy nature of the pattern and how it could feel modern and traditional at the same time. I chose to pull out the black in the mosaic for the countertop as a strong contrast to the whimsical blue cabinets. Finally I added a large plaid area rug in the adjoining keeping room to complement the American folk aesthetic introduced with the hexagon backsplash pattern.

The primary bedroom was a celebration of blue and white. I knew I wanted to use all white furniture and drapes to invoke the feeling of a sailboat—all white sails against a field of blue. I searched for a strong contrast for the walls against the sea of white furnishings and found the perfect backdrop. The en suite bathroom was clad in wood-trimmed walls accented with hydrangea blue ceilings and glass-front cabinets adding to the cottage appeal we wanted to achieve.

There are so many bedrooms in this house—after all, it is a vacation home. The homeowners knew they wanted plenty of room for friends to stay and the home has that in spades. On the basement level, I came up with different themes for each bedroom so it was an unique experience. The three main guest bedrooms were called Feather, Aspen, and Chestnut, with varying color schemes and patterns reflecting the different themes employed to decorate these spaces. A large bunk room was also located on this floor. These rooms all center on a large lower-level living room and billiard room for more fun and entertainment. Views to the water are highlighted by window placements in each room.

This project was such a joy to work on, not just for the stunning location and beautiful architecture. The real joy was collaborating on another project with family members I love to spend time with. When building a home from scratch, the client-designer relationship can go through many ups and downs along the way. But spending quality time with my niece and her family is one of my great pleasures. I am a lucky uncle indeed.

OPPOSITE: This large-scale Jacobean wallcovering has an impressive wow factor. We waited ten months for the charming blue-and-green toile fabric for the window treatments because it perfectly complements the wallcovering.

OPPOSITE: Birds alight in this study with turquoise and navy grass cloth wallcovering.

ABOVE: Avian art is an absolute favorite of mine and at the lake there are many different species of birds to enjoy. From hawks, cranes, and eagles, several different pieces of art are showcased in this lakeside home.

OPPOSITE: I knew I wanted to paint the kitchen cabinets blue, but I could not decide on the countertop material until I found this mosaic marble backsplash. The honed black pearl counters pull out the dark colors in the tilework.

ABOVE: A corner of the keeping room allows views and conversation to the breakfast room. The large round table boasts a lazy Susan, which works great for large family gatherings.

ABOVE: Sliding doors allow ease of indoor/outdoor living on the sunporch on cool days. The porch furniture is styled so much like the home's interior furnishings that you can forget you are living outside.

OPPOSITE: More blue is used in the keeping room adjacent to the kitchen for sofas and chairs with a dark green leather.

OPPOSITE: This wallcovering is contrasted with a blue-and-white pinstripe for a quieting visual effect.

RIGHT: Small tables are easily in reach to hold a morning cup of coffee.

BELOW: The blue-and-white wallcovering is a kaleidoscope pattern of interconnected stylized feathers. What could be a dizzying display of pattern is quieted by the white furniture and fabrics.

ABOVE: We reworked the floor plan of this home to create a larger bathing area. Glass-front cabinetry offers more storage and creates a more intimate bathroom. Curtains on the glass doors mean the client doesn't need to be too tidy when storing linens or bath supplies.

OPPOSITE: The vanity area was originally planned as built-ins for clothes, which the client didn't need because of a large walk-in closet. So, we placed a pair of sinks and vanity here instead. The repeating wallcovering from the bedroom gives visual continuity.

ABOVE: A guest bedroom has quiet bedding and colorful curtains. A vintage-style nightstand holds a charming lamp with wicker shade.

OPPOSITE: Details from the guest bedroom and bathroom showcase the comfort of this woodland lakeside home.

ABOVE: The powder room of the home has a shower for overflow guests. This room has no windows, so I selected a polished ceramic tile to reflect light from the hallway.

OPPOSITE: The basement bar is located by the door to the outside, where many water activities await guests and family.

A PASTORAL VISION

COLUMBIA, TENNESSEE

After twenty-five years in the interior design business, I am fortunate to have many repeat clients. Of those, I have a handful of clients for whom I have designed and decorated many homes. This current project was for one of the very few clients for whom I have completed more than five houses. This couple have been clients of mine for more than eighteen years. That history of working together was very necessary in order to build enough trust for them to give me carte blanche on most of the design decisions for a new house. For this pastoral vision, I worked with the architect Michael Katsaitis and the homeowners on a farm project that started from the raw earth to create a beautiful new dwelling.

Five years prior, we built, designed, and decorated a small guesthouse on their farm they named Sugar Moon Ridge. They nestled the Colonial-style cottage near a ridge of trees that overlooked a valley. Across the valley, they added a large barn with future plans for a main house. Finally the time came to build the main house and we started work in earnest to create a farmhouse with modern twists that spoke to the current times we live in.

The foyer was a study in geometry with applied moldings in white with raw white oak veneer inset panels. These panelized walls created an interesting foil to complement the couple's existing modern artwork you see throughout several rooms in the home. I wanted the house to feel like a farmhouse, yet not be too traditional or stuffy. The molding treatment as you enter this first room gave a hint of the modern touches to come.

The dining room, in my opinion, was one of the prettiest dining rooms I have ever created. I covered the walls in a dark aqua, large-gauge grass cloth to offset the light finishes of the table and chairs. I knew that the client had a large collection of china—one set from her mother and one set of her own—and she wanted to display all of the pieces. To hold all of this dishware, I designed a dish rack that runs from floor to ceiling, which allowed us to display all of her pieces. The sparkling dishes set among the coarse wallcovering would create a dazzling effect. I selected a large-scale flora-and-fauna fabric print on a white linen background to create a vivid contrast to the walls. The center of the room featured an open iron and crystal French-style chandelier.

The great room was connected to the foyer and kitchen as one wide-open space; large posts were added between the foyer and the great room to create a sense of division. I typically do not love vast, open spaces, because they lack a feeling of intimacy, so I often add obstructions in order to create more depth and a sense of mystery. If the view from one room to the next is obscured, then a visitor will be more motivated to look around and discover new rooms. This strategy was especially helpful in this space because the kitchen was also open to the great room. I wanted people to experience the spaces individually. Again, the owners' art came into consideration for the decor in this room, echoing the blue-and-aqua color scheme from the dining room.

A kitchen must be as functional as it is beautiful. Honestly, most of my clients do not use their kitchens as full, working, gourmet kitchens. But the client in this case was an avid cook. In all of the homes I have designed for her, she has exact requirements for the kitchen. We designed a very stylish "public"

ABOVE: I designed a floor-to-ceiling dish rack to house the client's dish collection as well as a dish collection from her mother.

OPPOSITE: The clients' modern painting in staccato-type brushstrokes mimics the movement of the window treatment fabric. The balance of energy between the windows and the artwork makes the room a spirited place to entertain friends and family.

kitchen and fashioned a working galley kitchen behind it. The "public" kitchen was all in white with a dramatic quartzite countertop with a matching full-slab backsplash. The effect was powerful and highlights the colors we used in the ancillary rooms of the house. For the working kitchen, I selected a dark navy cabinet with cement-colored subway tile to give it a feeling of utility. The rooms function well for her and are striking to see.

One of the main requests from the couple was to create a small den off the kitchen for watching TV. Because it will be just the two of them most of the time, they wanted a cozy, intimate spot to share their evenings together—they also wanted this spot to be conveniently located. There was a keeping room that the architect designed off the kitchen, but rather than decorating it as an extension of the kitchen, I decorated it more like a snug, which is what the British call small, intimate spaces to read a book, drink tea, or watch TV. The effect of the large furnishings, heavy window treatments, and ample upholstery hit all the marks on the clients' list.

The south wing of the house was dedicated to the owners' bedroom suite. A long, light-filled gallery led to the solarium or onward to the owners' private area. There was a small entry where I was able to create a special moment with a favorite bird-and-floral print that is echoed on the canopy over the bed.

I selected a warm gray for the wall paint and a soft turquoise textured fabric for the window treatments that matched a pair of club chairs. I repeated the wall color on the bathroom vanity cabinets to create continuity. A dramatic Asian-inspired wallcovering in peony trees and bamboo gave a touch of the Far East to the spa-like bathroom.

The solarium was the wife's idea because of her love of plants. Her goal was to have a lounge room where she could also overwinter plants and have a space for raising house plants and exotic flora. To this end, we decided against window treatments for the solarium and covered the floors in a large-format tile that looks like a Versailles-patterned wood parquet. This also helps to keep the floors in better shape since the pool is adjacent to this room and visitors will have to go through the solarium to access the powder room.

This beguiling farmhouse was the perfect denouement of a five-year development of rural farm land. From the outside, it stood proud and austere, but inside the open plan with modern flourishes continued to surprise and delight guests. They entered to enjoy the chic furnishings and finishes of a more urban-styled environment. This faithfully reflected the sense of sophistication from the homeowners and showed their personality and wanderlust.

OPPOSITE: A relatively neutral palette complements the clients' large painting of trees in shadow. Navy and cream colors, with accents of bright green, dial up the design. The feeling in the room is easy, elegant, and masculine.

OPPOSITE: The power of window treatments—this room absolutely would not look the same without them. A navy-and-white herringbone fabric with a beaded trim is both simple and elegant.

ABOVE LEFT: The detail of the window treatment shows the elaborately beaded band trim. The leaf-and-flower motif fits well into this elevated farmhouse.

ABOVE RIGHT: My love of birds shows in every job I design and decorate. This exotic-looking fowl fits right into my navy-and-green color scheme, adding style and whimsy to the living room mantel.

ABOVE: The back kitchen is finished with navy cabinetry. Open shelving allows a place to easily access dishes and serving trays for a busy at-home chef.

OPPOSITE: The kitchen is functional and beautiful. I splurged and installed the exotic quartzite counter material up the full backsplash to create more drama.

ABOVE: The snug is filled with comfortable furniture so it's inviting and cocooning. For this room, full-scale sofas and chairs and heavy drapes make a cozy room the couple never want to leave.

Dark green grass cloth wallpaper printed with a small white stripe pattern covers the walls.

I rarely match window treatments to furniture, as I prefer more contrast. However, in this case, the gold from the sofa and chair continues onto the drapes to great effect to keep the room serene and restful.

OPPOSITE: Yellow is a penetrating highlight used in details in several areas of the room.

OPPOSITE: The primary suite has ample natural light. Aqua is used on the drapes and bed canopy to echo the color of the pool just beyond the windows.

ABOVE: When I found this collection of vintage French oyster plates, I knew they belonged in this bedroom to complement the aqua throughout the room.

ABOVE: The main bathroom is another light-filled room in the house where I selected a favorite flora-and-fauna peony tree wallcovering. A warm gray for the vanity cabinets works well with the veined marble counters and floors.

OPPOSITE: A freestanding tub is a must in all new bathrooms and this one shines in front of the shower. What a restful spot to have a soak after a long day.

OPPOSITE: A marble-top table houses the clients' budding collection of plants, while an antique French-style mirror above the table reflects more daylight.

ABOVE: The conservatory sits just off the pool. The ample windows allow lots of light on sunny days. A favorite French-style armchair is dressed in a modern flame stitch, while the rest of the furnishings are neutral and calming.